Habitats

Oceans

Andrea Rivera

abdopublishing.com

Published by Abdo Zoom, a division of ABDO, PO Box 398166, Minneapolis, Minnesota 55439. Copyright © 2018 by Abdo Consulting Group, Inc. International copyrights reserved in all countries. No part of this book may be reproduced in any form without written permission from the publisher. Launch!™ is a trademark and logo of Abdo Zoom.

Printed in the United States of America, North Mankato, Minnesota.

092017

012018

Photo Credits: Alamy, iStock, Shutterstock

Production Contributors: Kenny Abdo, Jennie Forsberg, Grace Hansen, John Hansen

Design Contributors: Dorothy Toth, Neil Klinepier

Publisher's Cataloging-in-Publication Data

Names: Rivera, Andrea, author.

Title: Oceans / by Andrea Rivera.

Description: Minneapolis, Minnesota: Abdo Zoom, 2018. | Series: Habitats | Includes online resource and index.

Identifiers: LCCN 2017939241 | ISBN 9781532120695 (lib.bdg.) | ISBN 9781532121814 (ebook) | ISBN 9781532122378 (Read-to-Me ebook)

Subjects: LCSH: Oceans--Juvenile literature. | Marine biology--Juvenile literature. | Habitats--Juvenile literature.

Classification: DDC 577.7--dc23

LC record available at https://lccn.loc.gov/2017939241

Table of Contents

Science..4

Technology 10

Engineering 14

Art... 16

Math...................................... 18

Key Stats................................ 20

Glossary................................. 22

Online Resources....................... 23

Index 24

Science

Oceans are a kind of habitat.

Oceans are large bodies of salt water. Salt water covers about 70% of the Earth.

There are five oceans. They are the Pacific, Atlantic, Arctic, Indian, and Southern Oceans.

Mammals, fish, and other animals live in oceans. Blue whales are the largest mammals. They eat very tiny animals, called **krill**.

Technology

Ocean water is a great resource for humans.

But people get sick if they drink it. There is a process to separate salt from water.

Ocean water is put into large chambers. The sun heats the chambers.

The hot water **evaporates** and salt is left. Freshwater **condenses** on top of the chamber.

Engineering

Oceans are used for travel and **trade**. Early ships used oars and sails to move.

Today, engines help ships move even faster.

Art

There is an underwater museum in Mexico. More than 500 art pieces rest on the ocean floor.

Visitors can see them from a glass-bottom boat. Some visitors scuba dive to see the art!

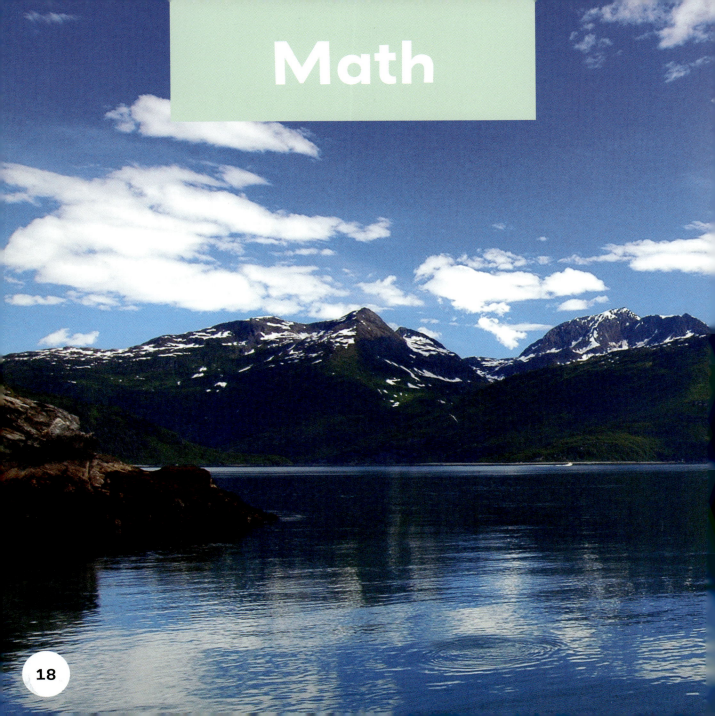

Oceans have high and low tides. The highest **tidal range** in the United States is in Alaska. It is 40 feet (12 m).

- Without oceans, the Earth could become too hot or too cold.

- All of the oceans in the world are connected. They cover about 70 percent of Earth's surface.

- The Pacific Ocean is the largest ocean in the world. The Arctic Ocean is the smallest.

- In the winter months, the Arctic Ocean is almost entirely covered in sea ice.

Glossary

condense – to cause to change from a gas to a liquid through cooling.

evaporate – to turn from liquid into gas.

krill – a small shrimp-like animal of the open seas.

mammal – a warm-blooded animal with fur or hair on its skin and a skeleton inside its body.

tidal range – the vertical difference between high tide and low tide. Tides are the rise and fall of sea levels caused by gravitational forces.

trade – the act of buying and selling goods.

Online Resources

For more information on oceans, please visit **abdobooklinks.com**

Learn even more with the Abdo Zoom STEAM database. Visit **abdozoom.com** today!

Index

Alaska 19

animals 8

freshwater 13

Mexico 16

motor 15

museum 16, 17

oceans 6

salt water 5, 11, 12, 13

scuba dive 17

ship 14

tides 19

trade 14

travel 14